21 DAYS

INTO

THE HEART OF JESUS

by

IAN JOHNSON

21 days
Into
The Heart of Jesus

Published by

His Amazing Glory Ministries
4 Ewing Road, RD4
Tuakau 2694
New Zealand

© Copyright 2009
Ian Johnson
ianjohn@xtra.co.nz

All Bible Quotes
New Living Translation 1997
Tyndale House: Wheaton III.
Unless otherwise stated

Dedicated to:

The Sisters of the Tyburn Monastery Bombay, who are an inspiration to me in their seeking of the face of Jesus. Their faces are an expression of all that is found in the heart of Jesus. They have shown what is possible if one becomes totally abandoned to Him.

21 DAYS INTO THE HEART OF JESUS

I invite you to take a journey into the heart of Jesus. This book is for personal use, or for use with groups in a retreat situation. It is based on the concept that if we come to Jesus, He will come to us. These very simple devotions are designed to open the door to intimacy with Jesus through experiencing His heart and entering the Glory Realm.

These principles of devotion are similar in structure to those used by St Ignatius Loyola in his 'Spiritual Exercises', first published in 1540. Those who used these for personal revival went on to spark significant moves of God in India, Malaysia, the Philippines, Indonesia and Japan. There was nothing in the spiritual exercises to suggest that the power of God would be released in signs, wonders and in raising the dead, but those who were influenced by them, ministered out of a pure love for Jesus, and saw some wonderful miracles as a result. Relationship sparked revival!

Nothing has changed, and personal revival still comes out of this relationship.

The power is not in the book but in your heart response to the moving of the Holy Spirit. Therefore this book is nothing more than simple words. If you let the Holy Spirit water these words, revival will surely come to your heart.

IAN JOHNSON - 2009

INDEX

Part one

Introduction

21 days of devotion.

Part Two

Jesus came down – *A life of humility*
Knowing Jesus – *It's not about us*
Grace and truth – *The pathway*
Abandoned – *The door into His heart*
Our view reveals our future –*Seated with Him*
Quotes that inspire.

Introduction

This book is not designed as a 'how to' manual, but rather as a workbook. It is a tool to assist the seeker who desires an intimate walk with Jesus to enter into the presence of the Master.

Why 21 days? Because it takes 21 days to form or break a habit, so the aim of this workbook is to help you form a habit of abandoned love 'for' and 'in' the heart of Jesus.

Each day there is a guided reading. A starting point if you like to help you set your mind on Jesus, begin to feel as He feels and to love as He loves.

If you will allow your heart to be touched by the Master, it is my prayer that after 21 days, a fire of revival will be lit. Revival must start in your heart. Revival is simply abandonment to the purposes of God.

Jesus said that if we see Him, we see the Father. Allow the Holy Spirit to open up your heart to the very heart of Jesus.

May God bless you on your journey as He has blessed many who have gone before.

Some of these men and woman, who discovered the passion and love found in the heart of Jesus, have changed the world forever. Many of these saints were persecuted, many were not understood, and some were even martyred. Without exception, these pioneers of faith, who turned the world upside down, were totally in love with Jesus, and abandoned to His purposes.

The journey is about relationship.
The pathways of the journey strengthen the heart.
Strong trees produce strong fruit.
Strengthened hearts produce a good harvest.
This is your invitation to see the heart of Jesus and
Then, abandon yourself to Him.

ENJOY THE JOURNEY!

How to use this book

Here's a thought! If we spend sixteen hours a day, thinking about our work, and how to spend our money...relaxing by the television and reading the daily news, and spend just five minutes with God...then the world will be 200 times more important to us than Jesus.

We all know that we need to spend time fostering our relationships and making them strong. Our relationship with Jesus is no different. The most common thing I discover in Christian circles is a lack of consistency. I meet many, who admit to having no prayer life at all.

Psalm 55:17 says, 'Evening and morning and noon will I pray and cry aloud; for He shall hear my voice.'

As you develop a habit of seeking Jesus, and become honest before Him, it will become clearer to you what the call on your life really is. Then your desire to spend more time with Him will begin to come naturally. In the early stages it will cost you, but it is imperative that you persevere to the point of breakthrough. As the flesh yields to an exciting heart relationship with Jesus, be on your guard. Determine to let nothing stop you from achieving your desire to have a heart on fire for Jesus.

> 'There is not in this world
> a kind of life more sweet,
> than that of a
> continual conversation
> with God.
> Those only can comprehend
> it, who practise
> and experience it.'
> *Brother Lawrence.*

Daily program

1) Commit your time to the Lord. Ask the Holy Spirit to reveal Jesus to you in a fresh way, so that you can experience Him in Heavenly places. This means when you seek Him, you seek Him outside of time.
2) Start with praise. Praise always leads us into the presence of Jesus. Just find an aspect of His character or nature, and praise Him for it. This will lead you into worship. Keep worshiping until He comes.
3) In His presence, read the daily devotion and meditate on the aspect of Jesus mentioned there. Allow the Holy Spirit to minister to you and open the eyes of your heart, then walk into what He shows you.
4) Wait for the Lord to speak to you personally. Remember you have two ears and one mouth. Just enjoy His presence.
5) The Lord may reveal things to you that need your attention in this time of waiting. If necessary, confess your trespasses and sins to the Lord allowing him to demonstrate His love.
6) Read the word, remembering that Jesus is the word made flesh. Allow

the Holy Spirit to reveal more of Jesus to you. As you read look at it from His side of eternity, not from your earthly realm.
7) Pray the word. If you can, speak the word out loud and allow it to become alive in your ears and your heart.
8) Come before the Lord with thanksgiving and especially thank Him for the aspect of Jesus you are looking at today.
9) Sing to the Lord ... Singing your way through the book of Psalms is a great way to release something fresh. Sing a new song, maybe one that you are hearing in Heaven.
10) Meditate on the Lord again. Simply go over all that the Lord has shown you today, breathing in the atmosphere of Heaven.
11) Stop and listen again for what the Lord is saying. Lean into the heart of Jesus and listen to His heartbeat. You will begin to pick up what it is He is saying.
12) Pray the prayer in the daily devotion. This prayer is only designed to be a beginning to what you will end up praying.
13) Worship the Lord and let the Holy Spirit lead you into deeper worship of Jesus.

14) Wait again and listen for His final instructions.
15) Use the workbook and answer the searching questions. Be honest and allow the Lord to guide your thinking.
16) Praise Him again just as you did in the beginning. Your heart will be full so let your lips speak it out.

The main concern of the devil
is to keep Christians from seeking
Jesus. He doesn't fear religion.
He doesn't fear prayer-less works.
He laughs at your toils.

But when you seek Jesus abandoning
yourself to the purposes of God,
the devil trembles.

*

'Prayer is nothing else
than being on terms
of friendship with God.'
Teresa of Avila

*'Few souls understand what God
would accomplish in them, if they were
to abandon themselves unreservedly
to Him and allow His grace to mould
them accordingly.'*
Ignatius Loyola

DAY ONE

COME TO ME AND I WILL GIVE YOU REST

Matthew 11: 28

Then Jesus said, "Come to me, all of you who are weary and carry heavy burdens, and I will give you rest. Take my yoke upon you. Let me teach you, because I am humble and gentle, and you will find rest for your souls. For my yoke fits perfectly, and the burden I give you is light."

'God of life, there are days when the burdens we carry chafe our shoulders and wear us down; when the road seems dreary and endless, the skies gray and threatening; when our lives have no music in them and our hearts are lonely, and our souls have lost their courage. Flood the path with light, we beseech you; turn our eyes to where the skies are full of promise.
Our hearts are restless, O Lord, until they rest in you.'
  St Augustine of Hippo 354AD 430AD

COME TO ME AND I WILL GIVE YOU REST

If today you are striving to be something great in God, but feel so weary, this isn't God's will for your life. Stop and rest a while with the Master. Take time to lean against His breast and listen to His heartbeat.
 John the Apostle had such a heart of love, because he had learnt to lean against the Master's heart while others were busy planning for tomorrow. Just rest in His love for you today, you won't miss His will for your life if you snuggle into His heart.

Come to me and I will give you rest.

What are the yokes that you are carrying? Remember that Jesus only did what the Father asked Him to do… no more. He doesn't expect any more from you. Write down some things that are burdening you. Take time to reflect on His yoke, and then think about the yokes you carry.

Write down the things you know for sure that the Lord has called you to do.

_____
_____

_____

Am I striving? If so, what is it that is driving me?

_____
_____
_____
_____
_____

If you have heard the Lord what will you do to change your situation.

It's time to praise the Lord.

Prayer

Jesus, I put off all other burdens and rest in You. Forgive me for striving. Can we just rest for a moment today? As we do, please tell me what is on Your heart, and I'll tell You what is on mine. Amen

Commit your journey to the Lord.

DAY TWO

COME AND I WILL QUENCH YOUR THIRST.

John 7:37-38
'On the last day, the climax of the festival, Jesus stood and shouted to the crowds, "If you are thirsty, come to me! If you believe in me, come and drink! For the Scriptures declare that rivers of living water will flow out from within."'

'We taste Thee, O Thou living Bread,
And long to feast upon Thee still;
We drink of Thee, the Fountainhead,
And thirst our souls from Thee to fill.'
Bernard of Clairvaux 1090 -1153 AD

'Praise God, from whom all blessings flow.
Praise Him, all creatures here below.
Praise Him above, ye heavenly host.
Praise Father, Son, and Holy Ghost.'
Thomas Ken 1674

COME AND I WILL QUENCH YOUR THIRST.

We fill our lives with activity designed to take our minds off this one thing… our thirst for the King. We drink from the waters of religion and form, yet notice we are still thirsty. There is a thirst that can only be quenched by the Lord. When we drink from His fountain our hearts come to life. Take some time today to drink deeply from the river of living water from His throne.

Have I become too busy to stop when I'm thirsty? Do I recognize that Jesus Christ is the only means to truly quench my thirst?

_____
_____
_____
_____
_____

When I drink, am I drinking deeply of Jesus or am I drinking the stagnant waters of religion?

_____
_____
_____
_____
_____
_____

What is the Lord saying to me about finding water that will always quench my thirst?

_____
_____
_____
_____
_____

It's time to praise the Lord.

Prayer

Jesus I am thirsty. I acknowledge that only You can satisfy my thirst. Today I come running in answer to Your request to, "Come!" Jesus please may I have a drink from the eternal river which flows from Your heart?. Amen

DAY THREE

180 DEGREES INTO THE HEART OF JESUS.

ACTS 3:19-20

'Now turn from your sins and turn to God, so you can be cleansed of your sins. Then wonderful times of refreshment will come from the presence of the Lord, and He will send Jesus your Messiah to you again.'

1 JOHN 1: 9

'But if we confess our sins to Him, He is faithful and just to forgive us and to cleanse us from every wrong. If we claim we have not sinned, we are calling God a liar and showing that His word has no place in our hearts.'

'Let us then not be ashamed to confess our sins unto the Lord. Shame indeed there is when each makes known his sins, but that shame, as it were, ploughs his land, removes the ever-recurring brambles, prunes the thorns, and gives life to the fruits which he believed were dead. Follow Him who, by diligently ploughing His field, sought for eternal fruit:' Ambrose of Milan

180 DEGREES INTO THE HEART OF JESUS

The journey into the heart of Jesus begins with a 180-degree turn around. Repentance is the starting point, and the place where the scripture says we receive refreshing from the presence of the Lord. Today is a turning point in your journey and a day in which you make a decision. It is a day to turn away from sin, and into the heart of Jesus.

Scripture recommends that we examine ourselves in God's presence. 1 Corinthians 11:28 says, 'Let a man examine himself, and so eat and drink of the cup.'

Do you acknowledge that your sins are an obstacle to intimacy with God?

As part of your reflection, take some time to think about your life... Is there anything between you and God right now?

_____
_____
_____
_____

Have I allowed myself to become too busy for a regular daily examination of my heart?

_____
_____
_____

What is the Holy Spirit saying about what I can put in place or change in my life to accomplish this special time with Him?

_____
_____
_____
_____
_____

It's time to praise the Lord.

Prayer

Jesus, I now wait upon You to show me my heart. Today I take time to turn away from the things that are displeasing to You, and to turn towards Your heart. Please forgive my sins and cleanse me. Today I choose to walk into Your heart.

DAY FOUR

THE VOICE OF JESUS IS LIKE NO OTHER.

JOHN 10:14-16

'I am the Good Shepherd; I know my own sheep, and they know me, just as my Father knows me and I know the Father. And I lay down my life for the sheep. I have other sheep too, that are not in this sheepfold. I must bring them also, and they will listen to my voice; and there will be one flock with one shepherd.'

'We believe that our God created this world for a purpose, namely to draw all of us into communion with Jesus and with one another. That means that at every moment of our existence, God is drawing us toward this goal and communicating with us.' St Ignatius Loyola 1491-1556

THE VOICE OF JESUS IS LIKE NO OTHER.

A good shepherd never leaves his sheep unattended. He is ever watchful and always speaking to them. It is because of His commitment to the sheep that we learn to hear the voice of the Master as He gently speaks to us. Jesus knows you, because you are a sheep of His pasture. He is calling you to come into green pastures and to dwell with Him beside still waters. It is all about ownership and the sooner we acknowledge that Jesus is Lord, which means He owns us, the sooner we will find life.

Do you hear the voice of God? Can you remember the times when God has clearly spoken to you? Write down how you best hear His voice.

_____
_____
_____
_____

When I hear the Lord Jesus speaking to me, do I let Him lead me into green pastures to rest with Him? What positive action can I take today to enter new pastures where I can learn to hear His voice?

_____
_____
_____
_____
_____
_____

It's time to praise the Lord.

Prayer

Jesus, thankyou that You are my Shepherd. I am comforted to know that You are leading me. Lord Jesus, I am listening to hear Your voice. I acknowledge that You are the Lord of my life. I am taking time right now to listen for Your instructions.

DAY FIVE

THE LIFE OF JESUS SUSTAINS US.

Acts 17:28
'*For in him we live, and move, and have our being;*'

'*Have you ever seen a painter able to produce a perfect picture while working on the top of an unstable table? No, I'm sure you have not. So to in your life, every movement of self, produces erroneous lines. In Jesus, there is life and it is as **He** paints the scapes of our life that perfect pictures come. Man by nature is restless. He does little, though it appears to be much. Remain in peace and move only when Jesus moves.*'
Madam Jeanne Guyon

'*Everything belongs to Him, and He will never release His right to anything. Free and intelligent creatures are His as much as those which are otherwise. He refers every unintelligent thing totally and absolutely to Himself, and He desires that His intelligent creatures should voluntarily make the same disposition of themselves.*'
Francois Fenelon 1651 -1715

THE LIFE OF JESUS SUSTAINS US.

Every breath we draw is a gift from God and today we are alive by His grace. He has given us a free will, but it is in our interest to yield that will to Him. It won't take away our freedom. It will in fact give us greater freedom as we learn that He is the Master and we are the canvas. The work of the Master is what people will stand in awe of, not the canvas.

Take some time to record your blessings in the following categories:

My life today.

DAY FIVE

The love that God has shown me in Jesus Christ.

_____
_____
_____
_____

How is the salvation I have received through Jesus Christ impacting my life today?

_____
_____
_____
_____
_____

It's time to praise the Lord'

Prayer

Jesus I yield to Your masterstrokes on the canvas of my life. Today it's exciting to know that You are in control, and that my life is in Your hands. Without You I wouldn't even have a life. I bow today before You Jesus. It is only You who sustains my life.

DAY SIX

ABANDONED TO THE VINE

John 15:5
'I am the vine; you are the branches. Those who remain in me, and I in them, will produce much fruit, for apart from me you can do nothing.'

John 15: 7- 8
'If you stay joined to Me and My words remain in you, you may ask any request you like, and it will be granted. My true disciples produce much fruit. This brings great glory to My Father.'

'What is abandonment? It is forgetting your past; it is leaving the future in His hands; it is devoting the present fully and completely to Jesus. Abandonment is being satisfied with the present moment, no matter what the moment contains. You are satisfied because you know that whatever the moment has, it contains – in that instant – God's eternal plan for you.' Jeanne Guyon

ABANDONED TO THE VINE

A branch cannot survive without its connection to the vine. Without it, it will wither and die. So it is with us. We are just branches connected into the True Vine. From this Vine we get everything that sustains our lives, and causes growth and the production of fruit. It should be a joy for us, to abandon ourselves to Jesus. "Remain in Me," Jesus said. Not just during times of prayer, or worship but every hour of the day and night. Abandoned to the Lord we produce a crop, first fruits for the Lord. Today make a decision to abandon yourself to Jesus.

Reflect on your life. Am I abandoning myself totally to Him?

_____
_____
_____
_____
_____

What sustains me? Am I living in the strength of my own personality or am I really connected to the Vine?

_____
_____
_____
_____
_____
_____

It's time to praise the Lord.

Prayer

Jesus, You are Life and it's Your life that sustains me. Therefore Lord I come to You with a heart abandoned to Your purposes for me. I draw deeply from the Vine and Your never-ending flow of life. Sustain me, fill me, and overflow me with Your grace, that I may become full of the life of God.

DAY SEVEN

COME AS A LITTLE CHILD

Matt 18:3-4

'Jesus called a small child over to Him and put the child among them. Then He said, "I assure you, unless you turn from your sins and become as little children, you will never get into the Kingdom of Heaven. Therefore, anyone who becomes as humble as this little child is the greatest in the Kingdom of Heaven.'

'It is needful to remain little before God and to remain little is to recognize one's childlikeness, and expect all things from God just as a little child expects all things from its father; it is not to be troubled by anything, not to try to make a fortune. Even among poor people, a child is given all it needs, as long as it is very little.
'To be little also means not to attribute to one's self the virtues that one practices, to acknowledge that God has placed these treasures in the hands of His little child so that the child can make use of them as needed, but always as the treasures of the good God.'
St Teresa of Lisieux

COME AS A LITTLE CHILD

To be a child before God is to recognise our total need of Him. A child relies on his Father for everything: for provision, for shelter, for comfort, for love, for guidance, for wisdom and for counsel. To be a child before God is to be loved and protected by the Father. I think at times we all grow to be bumptious teenagers in the Kingdom of God, but the longer we are Christians, the more we realise we know very little, and then as we grow older we return to being children again before God.

It is time to reflect on being a child of God. How do your reactions compare to that of a child?

_____
_____
_____
_____
_____
_____
_____
_____
_____

When you need wisdom or guidance how do you approach the Lord? Would you say it is childlike? Reflect on these things.

It's time to praise the Lord.

Prayer

Jesus, today I come as a very little child to You. My needs are great but I know that You will meet them because I am just a small child. Daddy I love You and I trust You. Please take my hand and lead me today, into the heart of Jesus. Amen.

DAY EIGHT

IN THE HEART OF JESUS WE FIND TEARS.

JOHN 11:35
'Jesus wept.'

LUKE 19:41
'As they came closer to Jerusalem Jesus saw the city ahead, He began to weep.'

'If Jesus' tears show us how much God loves the human community, and how much God grieves over our sorry state; if His tears reveal that God rescues us by being poured out like a sacrifice on our behalf, then surely the way for us to join in on God's mission is to throw ourselves into the torrent of God's outpouring, to be swept up and carried along by the sheer force of God's self-giving love.'
~ Tom Breidenthal

IN THE HEART OF JESUS WE FIND TEARS.

The heart of Jesus is found in the two verses above. His love and compassion moved Him to tears. Once He wept over His friend Lazarus and later over the city of Jerusalem. If we want to enter the heart of Jesus then we must see the human condition as He sees it and allow ourselves to be moved by the indifference of mankind to His ways. As we wait on the Lord our hearts will be moved, even as His heart was moved to tears. God the Father cannot resist tears; in fact the book of Psalms says He keeps all our tears in a bottle. Compassion is the hallmark of a heart relationship with Jesus. If we can't cry with Him, then how can we live in Him?

How do I honestly notice the plight of mankind? Is there compassion in my heart or judgement?

_____
_____
_____
_____

DAY EIGHT

What aspects of life touch me more than others? Do I allow the Lord to take me into this place?

_____
_____
_____
_____
_____
_____
_____\
_____
_____

It's time to praise the Lord.

Prayer

Jesus, today I ask for a heart like Yours, one that will weep over the condition of the men and woman around me. I present my tears to You today as an offering. I join in the flow of tears that come from Your heart of love for me and all my brothers and sisters.

DAY NINE

BECOMING A SON THROUGH ODEDIENCE

MARK 10:31-35

'Jesus' mother and brothers arrived at the house where He was teaching. They stood outside and sent word for Him to come out and talk with them. There was a crowd around Jesus and someone said, "Your mother and your brothers and sisters are outside, asking for you." Jesus replied, "Who is my mother? Who are my brothers?" Then He looked at those around Him and said, "These are my mother and brothers. Anyone who does God's will, is my brother and sister and mother."'

'Do you seek any further reward beyond that of having pleased God? In truth, you know not how great a good it is to please Him.'
John Chrysostom,

'My prayer for you is that you come to understand and have the courage to answer Jesus' call to you with the simple word 'yes'.'
Teresa of Calcutta

BECOMING A SON THROUGH ODEDIENCE

There is no service higher for Jesus, than that of obedience. Jesus was not denying His own family; indeed He was expressing a vision of a bigger family. We are told that all who are led by the Spirit of God are the sons of God; The Spirit of God will never lead us into disobedience. Therefore we become a son or daughter of God through obedience and doing the will of the Father. What is the Father's will? That as many as receive Jesus should become the sons of God and walk into the love of God as found in Jesus.

It is time to reflect on your obedience before the Lord. Take some time to write down areas you need to work on.

_____
_____
_____
_____

DAY NINE

Ask the Lord for grace that you may not be deaf to His call. Think about how you would react if the queen or king of a nation were to ask you to do something. What would your response be?

_____
_____
_____
_____

Relationship calls for a response. How can I be more open with the Lord today?_____

_____
_____
_____

It's time to praise the Lord.

Prayer

Jesus, thank you for allowing me the privilege of becoming a son of God, through the gift of Your salvation. Help me to become a doer of Your word, and to enter into the fullness of what it means to be in Your family.

DAY TEN

TO BE POOR IN SPIRIT IS TO BE RICH IN THE LORD.

☐Matthew 5:3

'Blessed are the poor in spirit, for theirs is the kingdom of heaven.'

'There is a terrible hunger for love. We all experience that in our lives - the pain, the loneliness. We must have the courage to recognize it. The poor you may have right in your own family. Find them. Love them.'
Teresa of Calcutta

Who are the poor in Spirit? The answer is anyone who recognises that without Jesus they are in absolute poverty. You can be a billionaire and be in total poverty of spirit. Conversely you can be the poorest of the poor financially, but because you are sold out to the purposes of God in Jesus, you are amongst the richest. Are you poor today or are you among the richest? Today we need to reflect on our riches or poverty of spirit and enter more fully into the heart of Jesus.

Spending time in His presence makes us rich.

TO BE POOR IN SPIRIT IS TO BE RICH IN THE LORD.

Who are the poor in Spirit who live near you? Let the Holy Spirit bring them to your attention.

_____
_____
_____
_____
_____
_____

As you reflect, consider where you are rich and where you are poor in your life.

_____
_____
_____
_____
_____
_____
_____
_____
_____
_____

DAY TEN

What is my measure of rich and poor?

_____
_____
_____
_____
_____

Is my thinking in line with Jesus' thinking?

_____
_____
_____
_____

It's time to praise the Lord.

Prayer

Jesus, I want to become rich. Today I want to enter into a revelation of the riches I have in You. Overwhelm me with Your love and grace. Please open my eyes to see the riches yet to be found in You.

DAY ELEVEN

'THE WAY' IS A PERSON NOT A PATTERN.

JOHN 14:6
'Jesus told him, "I am the Way, the Truth, and the Life. No one can come to the Father except through me"'

'Jesus does not give recipes that show the way to God as other teachers of religion do. He is Himself the Way.' Karl Barth

'Fundamentally, our Lord's message was Himself. He did not come merely to preach a Gospel; He Himself is that Gospel. He did not come merely to give bread; He said, "I am the bread." He did not come merely to shed light; He said, "I am the light." He did not come merely to show the door; He said, "I am the door." He did not come merely to name a shepherd; He said, "I am the shepherd." He did not come merely to point the way; He said, "I am the way, the truth, and the life."'... J. Sidlow Baxter

'THE WAY' IS A PERSON NOT A PATTERN.

Proverbs 16v25 says, 'There is a way that seems right to a man, but the ways thereof end in destruction.' We can run around in circles trying to find answers to our problems, or a way to solve the issues of life, but the truth of John 14 is, Jesus doesn't show us a way or give us a formula to find the way, He Himself is The Way.
The moment we realise that no amount of religious activity can take us any deeper into the heart of Jesus, this is the moment we enter into His rest. It is in that place of rest that we enter into The Way. Outwardly we can be very busy in our daily tasks, but if we have entered The Way, which is Jesus Himself, we have entered into rest. John Wesley said, "I am so busy, that I need to spend several hours in prayer, just to get everything done." He knew Jesus as 'The Way.'

Is my life driven by a set of rules, or am I walking in relationship with Jesus?

_____
_____
_____
_____

DAY ELEVEN

Take time to reflect on Jesus as The Way. What is the Holy Spirit saying to you now?

_____
_____
_____
_____
_____

It's time to praise the Lord.

Prayer

Jesus, today I cease from my own works and enter into The Way, which is You. Forgive me Lord for trying to work out my own way by using systems and programs, and neglecting the only Way which is You Jesus, and only You.

DAY TWELVE

SEEING JESUS IS THE CLIMAX OF OUR PILGRIMAGE.

Colossians 3:1-4

'Since you have been raised to new life with Christ, set your sights on the realities of Heaven, where Christ sits at God's right hand in the place of honor and power. Let Heaven fill your thoughts. Do not think only about things down here on Earth. For you died when Christ died, and your real life is hidden with Christ in God. And when Christ, who is your real life, is revealed to the whole world, you will share in all His glory.'

'The climax of all heavenly joy and wonder is "Seeing Jesus" and worshiping Him who saved us by His blood. Soon after entering the gates of the Heavenly City, our first desire is to see Jesus, and reverently gaze with love and devotion upon the Lord of all creation.' H.A. Baker "Visions beyond the Veil."

SEEING JESUS IS THE CLIMAX OF OUR PILGRIMAGE.

Our true home is Heaven and our true King is Jesus. Our lives are designed to be lost in a heavenly gaze. And our hearts are called to one thing and that is the worship of Jesus, hidden in His heart, wrapped in His glory and enthralled by His majesty. This is "Real life." Today let your heart be captured by thoughts of "seeing Jesus" and seeing His heart.

Meditate on your true home in Heaven. Write down some of your thoughts.

_____
_____
_____
_____
_____
_____
_____
_____

DAY TWELVE

Now ask the Lord to show you your home in the heart of Jesus. Write down what He shows you.

_____
_____
_____
_____
_____
_____
_____
_____

Spend lots of time in worship.

Prayer

Jesus, today I meditate on the fact that my home is with You in Heaven. The first thing I have to say is, "Thank you for calling me into your home. I want to spend time today, just worshiping You. I want my life to be seen only in You, I want to be hidden in Your glory. Thank you that my real life is in You. Help me to see only You and to be filled with Your majestic presence."

DAY THIRTEEN

RECEIVING THE POWER TO UNDERSTAND HIS LOVE

Ephesians 3:18-19

'May you have the power to understand, as all God's people should, how wide, how long, how high, and how deep His love really is. May you experience the love of Christ, though it is so great you will never fully understand it. Then you will be filled with the fullness of life and power that comes from God.'

John 15:9

'I have loved you even as the Father has loved me. Remain in my love.'

'Lead us to the wild solitary spot in our own hearts where we may encounter Your gift of fiery love and see the gracious way You look upon us from the cross. Help us to open ourselves to Your limitless love, which holds nothing back from us   Francis of Assisi

THE POWER TO UNDERSTAND HIS LOVE

Every time we think we have come to an understanding of the love that Christ has for us we are surprised again. Today we meditate on this great love, the love that looks upon us from the cross that looks down through the centuries and falls upon us, right where we are today. His love is what caused Him to pay such a great price on the cross, and His love is what causes Him to continue His pursuit of our attention. We will never fully understand His love in this life, but I think when we get to Heaven we will be amazed at its depth.

Meditate on the love of Jesus. Write down how His love has impacted your life.

_____
_____
_____
_____
_____
_____
_____

DAY THIRTEEN

Meditate on the cross and write down your thoughts about its expression of love.

_____
_____
_____
_____

How can I open myself to this love in a greater way?

_____
_____
_____
_____

Worship should come easy.

Prayer

Jesus, every time I think of Your love, I am overwhelmed. Help me see what You saw, and continue to see, from the cross. I know that this prayer will ruin me forever, but Lord unless I understand the love that flows from Your heart, I will never fulfil the mission You have for me. Lord, please grant me the power to understand more fully the depths of Your love.

DAY FOURTEEN

IN HIS PRESENCE WE SEE HIS GLORY.

John 11:40

'Jesus responded, "Didn't I tell you that you will see God's glory if you believe?"'

John 1:14

'So the Word became human and lived here on earth among us. He was full of unfailing love and faithfulness, and we have seen His glory, the glory of the only Son of the Father.'

'A man can no more diminish the glory of Jesus by refusing to worship Him than a lunatic can put out the sun by scribbling the word 'darkness' on the walls of his cell.'
C.S. Lewis

IN HIS PRESENCE WE SEE HIS GLORY'

When we enter into the heart of Jesus we are confronted with His glory. The glory of God is the atmosphere of Heaven, just as air is the atmosphere of Earth. Today as we seek Jesus and consider His glory, the atmosphere will change. Heaven will invade the dark recesses of your heart. Wherever Jesus is, there is a transforming glory. Open up your heart today to the possibilities of an invasion of glory and receive the fullness of the Godhead revealed in Him.

Spend some time asking to see some new aspect of God's glory as expressed in Jesus. You may need to come back to this question time and time again, because there is so much of Jesus to discover.

_____
_____
_____
_____
_____
_____
_____
_____

DAY FOURTEEN

Seeing the glory of Jesus brings transformation to our lives and surroundings. Write down some areas you would like to see transformed. Then spend some time reflecting on the glory of Jesus.

_____
_____
_____
_____
_____
_____
_____

Worship Jesus and the fullness of His glory.

Prayer

Jesus let me walk into the fullness of who You are. Help me see Your glory. Invade me with Your glory. Jesus I'm expecting a change of atmosphere and a transforming miracle as I enter into Your presence. I wait upon You now Jesus, please open my eyes.

DAY FIFTEEN

HAVING A HEART TO FISH FOR SOULS

Matthew 4:18-20

'One day as Jesus was walking along the shore beside the Sea of Galilee, He saw two brothers, Simon, also called Peter, and Andrew, fishing with a net, for they were commercial fishermen. Jesus called out to them, "Come, be my disciples, and I will show you how to fish for people"'

'I wish to wait for His promise which is never unfulfilled, just as it is promised by the Lord: "Many shall come form the east and west and sit at the table with Abraham, Isaac and Jacob." Just as we believe that believers shall come from the whole world, so for this reason one should, in fact fish well and diligently, just as the Lord teaches, saying, "Follow me and I will make you fishers of men." So it behoves us to spread our nets, that a vast multitude and throng might be caught for God.'
St Patrick of Ireland

HAVING A HEART TO FISH FOR SOULS

The dearest thing we find in the heart of the Lord is His desire to touch all of mankind. To do this He employs fishermen. If we are to truly enter into the heart of Jesus we will need to be filled with passion for souls, the same passion that led our Master to the cross. There is a lot of room in Heaven, and many rooms yet to be filled. As you lean today against the Master's breast, hear His heartbeat for the man at the bus stop, the woman in the mall and the young people in the park, and cast out your net.

Ask the Lord for His heart toward people you know. Write down His response and begin to seek ways of expressing His heart towards them.

_____
_____
_____
_____
_____
_____
_____
_____

DAY FIFTEEN

Fishing requires patience. The Lord once spoke to me and said, "My people give up too soon when it comes to fishing for souls." Take some time to reflect on how you could be more patient in your fishing for men. Write it down.

_____
_____
_____

It's time to worship the Lord.

Prayer:

Jesus, I hear Your call and I will follow. Help me to consistently hear Your heartbeat for the lost, and as I listen Lord, please give me the grace to cast out my net, and bring in a vast haul for You, so that Heaven may be full of those You have called to be Your sons and daughters.

DAY SIXTEEN

OUR MISSION IS RELEASED IN HIS COMPASSION

Matthew 9:35-37

'Jesus travelled through all the cities and villages of that area, teaching in the synagogues and announcing the Good News about the Kingdom. And wherever He went, He healed people of every sort of disease and illness. He felt great compassion for the crowds that came, because their problems were so great and they didn't know where to go for help. They were like sheep without a shepherd. He said to His disciples, "The harvest is so great, but the workers are so few. So pray to the Lord who is in charge of the harvest; ask Him to send out more workers for His fields."'

'I do not believe in the salvation of anyone who does not try to save others.'
St. John Chrysostom;

OUR MISSION IS RELEASED IN HIS COMPASSION

Compassion is expressed in many ways, through prayer, through service or through the word of faith released into hopeless situations. However true compassion is found in the heart of Jesus and when we see through His heart, compassion will flow out of us into our very needy world. Today as we meditate on the harvest, allow the compassion of Jesus to be your launching pad into the harvest field.

Take some time to feel the Lord's compassion for the people around you. Write down what He is saying to you.

_____
_____
_____
_____
_____
_____
_____
_____

DAY SIXTEEN

How has this time affected your desire to reflect the compassion of the Lord?

_____
_____
_____
_____
_____

What will you commit to do to reflect this compassion? Let the Lord be your guide. What is He asking you to do?

_____
_____
_____
_____

It's time to worship the Lord.

Prayer

Jesus, fill my heart with the compassion that is in Your heart and let me see the harvest from the cross, as You see it. Overflow me with desire for the lost, and show me my part in this harvest

DAY SEVENTEEN

ONE IN JESUS, ONE WITH EACH OTHER.

Matthew 18:19-20
'I also tell you this, If two of you agree down here on earth concerning anything you ask, My Father in Heaven will do it for you. For where two or three gather together because they are Mine, I am there among them.'

John 17:21
' My prayer for all of them is that they will be one, just as You and I are one, Father—that just as You are in me and I am in You, so they will be in us, and the world will believe You sent me.'

'There were two old men who had dwelt together for many years, who never quarreled. One said to the other, "Let us pick a quarrel with one another, even as other men do." "I know not how to quarrel," said the younger. To which the older replied, "Set then this brick in the middle and say this is mine, to which I will say, 'No it is mine!', from whence quarreling will begin." So they

placed the brick in the midst, and one said, "This is mine!" to which the other said, "If this be so, then take it and go thy way in peace." So they were unable to quarrel.'

Sayings of the Desert fathers

ONE IN JESUS, ONE WITH EACH OTHER.

As we enter into the heart of Jesus we find unity, the same unity that is between the Father and the Son and the Holy Spirit. In His last major prayer, as recorded in John 17, we see the desire of His heart, "That they may be one". Today as we meditate on Jesus think about the unity He longs to see between us. Take some time to ask the Lord to show us the importance of unity, and then seek unity with all of the body of Christ.

Unity, is not agreeing with everything everyone says, rather it is coming to a working agreement. In what areas do you need to come into agreement with your brothers or sisters?

_____
_____

DAY SEVENTEEN

Take some time to reflect on the part of the 'Lord's prayer' that says, "Forgive those who trespass against us." Is there any one you need to forgive? What steps are you taking today to make things right?

_____
_____
_____
_____
_____

It's time to worship the Lord.

Prayer

Jesus, please help me to see where I need to forgive, and give me the will to do it. I pray for unity between myself and all my brothers and sisters. As I come into unity with You and Your children I am expecting a blessing, because You have promised it in Psalm 133.

DAY EIGHTEEN

WISDOM AND KNOWLEDGE ARE FOUND IN JESUS.

Colossians 2:2-3
'My goal is that they will be encouraged and knit together by strong ties of love. I want them to have full confidence because they have complete understanding of God's secret plan, which is Christ Himself, in Him lie hidden all the treasures of wisdom and knowledge.'

'The best and most beautiful things in the world cannot be seen or even touched. They must be felt with the heart.' Helen Keller

'When we are at our wit's end we are at the beginning of God's wisdom.' Oswald Chambers

' Life in Christ is the only life built from Heaven earthward and from the inside out.' Calvin miller

WISDOM AND KNOWLEDGE ARE FOUND IN JESUS.

I have a saying and this is it. "Whatever the question, the answer is found in Jesus," and I believe it. God heard the cry of the human heart and He sent Jesus. Most people fumble around trying to solve their issues in their own strength. However the end of such fumbling is disappointment. Hidden in the heart of Jesus is everything you will ever need.

What questions are burning in your heart today? Ask the Lord to bring wisdom into your situation. Record what He is saying to you today.

DAY EIGHTEEN

Think about how the Lord has given you wisdom and knowledge in the past. Record the way He led you into this wisdom.

_____
_____
_____
_____
_____
_____

Take some more time to honour the Lord with your expectant waiting heart.

_____
_____
_____
_____
_____

It's time to worship the Lord.

Prayer

Jesus, there is so much I don't know, but I trust You and I know that every thing that I will ever need is found in You. Lord I am at the end of my self and I accept Your wisdom today.

DAY NINETEEN

LIFE IS FOUND IN JESUS.

John 11:25-26

'Jesus told her, "I am the resurrection and the life. Those who believe in me, even though they die like everyone else, will live again. They are given eternal life for believing in me and will never perish."

'The Lord once declared that He alone is life. All other creatures have 'borrowed life.' The Lord has life in Himself. That life, which is in Him, also carries with it His nature. This is the unique life, which He desires to give you. He wishes to make you a partaker of His divine life. The only way this becomes practical experience to you is by dying to self. So that the life of God can be substituted in its place '
Jeanne Guyon

LIFE IS FOUND IN JESUS.

When we consider our life we often think of it as our own possession, but the way it is described by the quote above is that it is borrowed life. Our real life will begin when we are full of resurrection life. That doesn't have to be when we die, because as we press into the heart of Jesus we receive His life in our mortal bodies. Then we come to the place of realizing that whether we live or die, our life is in Christ. To know Jesus is to experience His fullness. Jesus Himself is life. The Bible says that He holds all things together by His word.

Consider the life of Jesus. Think about the resurrection power that dwells in you as a result of His life. What does this mean to you?

_____
_____
_____
_____
_____
_____

DAY NINETEEN

Right now 'Life' runs through your body. It is the Life that sustains the universe. Write down your thoughts as you meditate on this Life.

_____
_____
_____
_____
_____
_____

It is time to worship the Lord.

Prayer

Jesus I thank you for my life. I yield it to You, and in so doing I receive Your life, which is resurrection life. I give my body to You as a living sacrifice and with it all my dreams, ambitions and plans, because I know that true life is only found in You.

DAY TWENTY

GOD ALLOWS US IN. HOW WONDERFUL HE IS!

John 1:1-5 'In the beginning the Word already existed. He was with God, and He was God. He was in the beginning with God. He created everything there is. Nothing exists that He didn't make. Life itself was in Him, and this life gives light to everyone. The light shines through the darkness, and the darkness can never extinguish it.'

John 1:14 'So the Word became human and lived here on earth among us. He was full of unfailing love and faithfulness. And we have seen His glory, the glory of the only Son of the Father.'

'Our problem is this: we usually discover Him within some denominational or Christian ghetto. We meet Him in a province and, having caught some little view, we paint Him in smaller strokes. The Lion of Judah is reduced to something kittenish because our understanding cannot, at first, write larger definitions' Calvin Miller

'The Lord ate from a common bowl, and asked the disciples to sit on the grass. He washed their feet, with a towel wrapped around His waist - He, who is the Lord of the Universe.' Clement of Alexandria

GOD ALLOWS US IN. HOW WONDERFUL HE IS.

He is the Creator of the Universe and the Master of all. This Jesus whom we serve is indeed the living God. What a privilege to come and rest at His feet, have Him speak to us and hear Him share His thoughts and His heart with us. Take the time now to acknowledge Jesus as God. As the Word becomes flesh in our hearts, the Glory of God will be manifest for all men to gaze upon.

Take some time to see how wonderful He is. Write down some things that come to mind when considering this.

_____
_____
_____
_____
_____
_____
_____
_____
_____
_____
_____

DAY TWENTY

How do you see Jesus? Is He the Creator of the Universe to you? Is He the one who sits upon the throne for ever, or is He gentle Jesus meek and mild?

Write down some new aspect of Jesus' character you have seen today.

_____
_____
_____
_____
_____
_____
_____
_____

Now let's worship the Lord.

Prayer:

Jesus, Master and Creator of all, I adore You today in all Your glory, and marvel that I can lean upon Your bosom, and have You love me. My heart and my flesh cry out in worship to You, oh Great Majesty and Lord. Jesus I love You.

DAY TWENTY- ONE

JESUS, MIGHTY GOD, WE FALL DOWN AT YOUR FEET.

Revelation 1 9 -18 'I am John, your brother. In Jesus we are partners in suffering and in the Kingdom and in patient endurance. I was exiled to the island of Patmos for preaching the word of God and speaking about Jesus. It was the Lord's Day, and I was worshiping in the Spirit. Suddenly, I heard a loud voice behind me, a voice that sounded like a trumpet blast. It said, "Write down what you see, and send it to the seven churches: Ephesus, Smyrna, Pergamum, Thyatira, Sardis, Philadelphia, and Laodicea."

'When I turned to see who was speaking to me, I saw seven gold lamp stands. And standing in the middle of the lamp stands was the Son of Man. ☐ He was wearing a long robe with a gold sash across His chest. His head and His hair were white like wool, as white as snow, His eyes were bright like flames of fire. His feet were as bright as bronze refined in a furnace, and His voice thundered like mighty ocean waves. He held seven stars in His right hand, and a sharp two-edged sword came from His mouth. And His face was as bright as the sun in all its brilliance.

'When I saw Him, I fell at His feet as dead. *But He laid His right hand on me and said, "Don't be afraid. I am the First and the Last. I am the living one who died. Look, I am alive forever and ever. And I hold the keys of death and the grave."'*

There are no quotes or words to say today, just a shout of praise and a glimpse of His glory that causes us to fall face down. For in the journey into His heart we have discovered the Living God full of glory and wonder. Amen and amen.

How has coming into the heart of Jesus impacted your thinking?

_____
_____
_____
_____
_____
_____
_____
_____
_____
_____
_____
_____
_____
_____
_____
_____
_____
_____
_____
_____

What Next?

Your journey has not ended it has just begun. In the book of Revelation, we read that the twenty four elders and the living creatures, who are constantly before the throne, fall down and cry out in worship, "Holy, Holy, Holy," every time they look upon the throne. This tells us that there is so much of God to know and worship. If every time *they* look at Him they see something new to inspire fresh worship, then we too have so much more to discover about Jesus. The more you look for Him, the more you will find Him. Amen.

'If I am a child of God, then of necessity my heart is already the temple of God, and Christ is already within me. What is needed therefore is only that I recognise His presence and yield fully to His control.'
Hannah Whitall Smith

Ian & Joye Johnson

**Are leaders and founders of
'His Amazing Glory ministries'
in
Auckland, New Zealand.**

www.hisamazinggloryministries.org

They have a heart to see revival come to the lives of individuals in the body of Christ. They travel under the banner of 'His Amazing Glory Ministries' to encourage the body of Christ, to seek the Glory of God and the release of an end time harvest.

Consider having Ian and Joye Johnson minister in your church or Conference in:-

**Intimacy with Jesus Conferences
Glory Miracles services
Evangelistic Crusades**

For speaking enquiries
E-mail ianjohn@xtra.co.nz
His Amazing Glory Ministries
4 Ewing Road RD4
Tuakau 2694
New Zealand

ABOUT THE AUTHOR

Saved in 1977 as a result of a face to face encounter with Jesus; Ian Johnson has always sought to live in a life of encounter and intimacy with the Lord. With a heart for history, Ian has discovered that in every century the Church has demonstrated the supernatural. He has made it his mission to communicate the mystical and supernatural realm of the Kingdom of God to this current generation.

Ian has been in ministry for over 25 years having pioneered and led Churches in the South Auckland area of New Zealand.

Ian and Joye Johnson travel as itinerant ministers speaking in Churches and conferences in NZ, Australia and the nations. Currently Ian is on the leadership team at Horizon Church in Auckland, New Zealand.

For speaking enquiries
E-mail ianjohn@xtra.co.nz
His Amazing Glory Ministries
4 Ewing Road RD4
Tuakau 2694
New Zealand

OTHER TITLES BY IAN JOHNSON

Glory to Glory
A Journey of Intimacy & Worship

The Miracles of Francis Xavier
Also published as:
Man On A Mission.

Anzac's Israel & God
The ANZAC legacy & modern Israel

Gems from Heaven
A collection of quotes from the ministry of Ian Johnson

All titles Available From

His Amazing Glory Ministries
4 Ewing Road RD4 Tuakau
2694, New Zealand.

Ph (09)2368126
E-mail ianjohn@xtra.co.nz

His Amazing Glory Ministries

Ian & Joye Johnson travel the nation & the nations opening realms of glory. Based at Horizon Church in Auckland New Zealand where they are part of the governmental leadership team. Ian speaks at Church and conference's as a sought after prophetic ministry.

**To book Ian Johnson for Church or Conference speaking engagements contact the ministry by e-mail
ianjohn@xtra.co.nz**

Made in the USA
Middletown, DE
07 November 2016